David Van Horne

A History of the Reformed Church in Philadelphia

David Van Horne

A History of the Reformed Church in Philadelphia

ISBN/EAN: 9783743358744

Manufactured in Europe, USA, Canada, Australia, Japa

Cover: Foto ©Lupo / pixelio.de

Manufactured and distributed by brebook publishing software (www.brebook.com)

David Van Horne

A History of the Reformed Church in Philadelphia

OF THE

Reformed Church in Philadelphia.

BY

REV. DAVID VAN HORNE.

PUBLISHED BY REQUEST.

PHILADELPHIA:
REFORMED CHURCH PUBLICATION BOARD,
907 ARCH STREET.
1876.

PREFACE.

The substance of the following history was embraced in two discourses, delivered in the First Reformed Church of Philadelphia, on Race Street below Fourth Street, on Sunday, July 2d, 1876, at the hours of morning and evening service, respectively. The occasion, as need hardly be stated, was the celebration of the One Hundredth Anniversary of the Declaration of American Independence. The work was undertaken in compliance with a request made by the Church Synods, and the National Centennial Commission, that the various Christian congregations should make account of the occasion, by preparing sketches of their past histories, as a suitable contribution to our Centennial celebration.

There seemed to be a special fitness for the attempt in the present instance, in view of the length of time over which the history ran—extending almost half a century into the ante-revolutionary period. The location of this church, within hearing distance of the old bell that rang out the peals of liberty in 1776, and not far distant from the grounds of the great International Exposition of 1876, afforded another significant reason why the work should be undertaken.

The desire, expressed by many persons, that the matter presented should be thrown into a printed form for preservation, has led to the publication of this little volume. The history is divided into two parts, corresponding to the two discourses; with the addition of the introductory description of early German immigration, the school regulations, and the sketch of the church colonies. The work is now given to the public with the hope that it may be useful to the cause of the Redeemer and be blessed to the encouragement of the congregation for which it was originally prepared.

The work of preparation has not been performed without difficulty. Ancient church records, and a confused mass of yellow and faded parchments and papers with German hieroglyphics upon them, presented themselves for scrutiny, and the effort to unravel the thread of narrative from them, was like the search for the "lost manuscript."

But, thanks to the authors of Reformed Church literature, among whom Dr. H. Harbaugh must be first mentioned, and to brethren who kindly gave assistance by suggestions, and aid in translating the documents, the work in this brief form is now completed. Thanks are due, and are hereby tendered to Revs. S. R. Fisher, D. D., A. Romich, and Messrs. Thompson Wescott, J. W. Jordon, I. D. Rupp, Samuel H. Bibighaus, J. G. Alburger, and F. E. Vandersloot.

Philadelphia, October 1, 1876.

CONTENTS.

PART I.

	PAGE
Leaving the Fatherland,	7
Perils by Land and Sea,	10
Mr. Weiss organizes the Church in Philadelphia,	15
The Ministry of Mr. Bœhm,	19
Mr. Schlatter Installed as Pastor,	21
The First Church Building,	23
The Organization of the First Synod,	25
The Controversy between Mr. Schlatter and Mr. Steiner,	26
The First Rival Congregation,	28
The Ministry of Mr. Steiner,	31
Ancient School Regulations,	32
The Ministry and Fall of Mr. Rothenbühler,	38
The Second Rival Congregation,	40
Dr. Weyberg Installed as Pastor,	41
The Charter, and Second Church Building,	42
Revolutionary Incidents,	43
Rev. Mr. Winkhaus Installed as Pastor,	47
Dr. Hendel succeeds to the Pastorate,	48
Second Pestilence of Yellow Fever,	49

CONTENTS.

PART II.

	PAGE.
State of the Congregation in 1800,	53
Loyalty of Pastors and People,	54
Description of the Second Church Building,	56
Origin of the Parochial and Sunday-Schools,	58
The Pastorate of Dr. Helffenstein,	63
Troubles in Changing to the English Language,	64
The Party in Favor of English Withdraw,	5
The Germans Withdraw,	68
Rev. Mr. Finney Introduces English Exclusively,	71
The Old Grave Yard in Franklin Square,	73
Rev. Mr. Sprole Installed as Pastor,	76
Pastorate of Dr. Berg,	77
Prosperity of the Church,	78
Public Debates,	80
Dr. Berg's Farewell,	81
The Ministry of Rev. Mr. Reid,	85
Dr. Bomberger Installed as Pastor,	85
The Tercentenary Convention,	86
Reformed Churches in Philadelphia in 1876,	89
Ecclesiastical Connection and Retrospect,	94
Concluding Reflections,	102

PART I.

A HISTORY

OF THE

Reformed Church in Philadelphia,

Between the Years 1727 and 1800.

PSALM 77: 5.
"I have considered the days of old, the years of ancient times."
„Ich denke der alten Zeit, der vorigen Jahre."

Leaving the Fatherland.

NEARLY one hundred and fifty years ago when Philadelphia was little more than a frontier village on the borders of that primitive forest, that stretched from the Gulf of Mexico, to Hudson's Bay, and from the Atlantic coast to the great unexplored prairies of the West, a friendless people came hither seeking to establish for themselves, homes in the Provinces of North America. Far from their fatherland, these refugees from Germany, Switzerland and France, landed on the American coast to commence anew their struggles for "life, liberty and the pursuit of happiness." They were, many of them, victims of persecution. Driven from their homes, stripped of nearly all their possessions, unacquainted even with the language spoken in the New World, they began their patient labors for the future, with only their trust in God, and their strong arms to sustain them. No poet has yet appeared to write of their toils and sacrifices, and tell the world their woes. All the history that we have of them, are the colonial records giving notice' of their arrival, and a few letters and state papers relating to their settlements. And yet, but few people have undergone greater sufferings, or sacrificed more for their religion.

The forefathers of the Reformed Church in the United States, came largely from the Palatinate, a district of Germany, situated in the middle Rhine region, and consequently on the borders of France. From the dawn of the great Reformation in the sixteenth century, this people had adopted the Reformed faith, and thus were marked victims of Romish persecution. And as their territory lay nearest to Rome, of all the Protestant Germanic States, the heaviest blows of the enemy fell upon them. Their fair land was again and again the theatre of desolating war.

In former years they had befriended other fugitives from Papal persecution, and this may have caused their enemies to be more cruel and relentless in their attacks upon them. To them, the French Reformed people known as Huguenots, had previously fled for refuge, when Louis XIV. followed up the scenes that resulted from the St. Bartholomew massacre, with armies that swept over the land to exterminate all the people who would not bow at the decrees of the Pope. When in 1685, the edict of Nantes was revoked, the furies of desolating war were again let loose, and bloodshed and devastation followed in their track. Huguenots and Palatinates alike were at last forced to flee before the persecutions; and thus friendless and homeless, they came to this asylum of the oppressed. It is estimated that between the years of 1702 and 1727, as many as forty or fifty thousand people fled from the district where the merciless troops of Louis XIV. under Turenne, were burning the houses and destroying the crops, and pursuing the inhabitants with indiscriminate slaughter. Stripped of everything, masses of these refugees made their way to England and other countries. It is stated that in July, 1709, there arrived at London, over thirteen thousand German Protestants, over six thousand of whom were sent by the Queen to the colonies in America.

Perils by Land and Sea.

One colony of them sent by Queen Anne to Schoharie, N. Y., in 1709, endured great sufferings and privations. They were six months on the voyage to New York, and seventeen hundred died on the passage, or soon after landing. Upon removing to Livingston Manor, near Albany, the leaders of the colony came into conflict with Governor Hunter, who had employed them to raise hemp and manufacture tar, to repay the English government for their transportation. Late in the Autumn of 1712, one hundred and fifty families started through the forest for Schoharie, some sixty miles distant. They were soon overtaken with a heavy fall of snow, and as they had no horses, were obliged to drag their effects on rude sleds by hand. After three weeks of toil and exposure, they arrived at the territory granted them by the Queen, and commenced their settlement. But after ten years of hard labor, they learned that there was a defect in their titles, and they lost both land and improvements.

In the Spring of 1723, thirty-three families under the lead of Conrad Weiser, undertook the perilous adventure of descending the Susquehanna river on rafts. No record remains of that adventurous voyage. The imagination alone can picture the scene. On the swift turbulent waters, swollen by the spring-rains, their rude unwieldy raft sped on. Overhanging them were the river bluffs covered with giant forest trees, or deep dark thickets in whose unfriendly recesses, the treacherous savage, or fierce wild beast might be lurking for their prey.

" It was a band of exiles; a raft as it were from the shipwrecked Nation, scattered along the coast, now floating together,
Bound by the bonds of a common belief, and a common misfortune."

Many of these emigrants fell into the hands of greedy and unscrupulous speculators, who consigned them to ship captains, to be crowded into the holds of the vessels in immense cargoes, with the understanding that they were to be stinted in food on the passage, and put ashore at any point that might be most convenient to their landing. In the winter of 1731-2, there came an appeal directed to Rev. Mr. Weiss, who was then supposed to be at Philadelphia, from a ship-load of these ill-fated immigrants who had sailed from Rotterdam for Philadelphia. They had been half starved and plundered by a Captain Labb, and the details of their treatment on the vessel are shocking in the extreme. They were thankful to escape with their lives, and ended their narrative with these words: "At last it pleased Almighty God to send us a sloop, which brought us to Homes Hole, near Martha's Vineyard." From that point they wrote for aid to come to this city, as they were then in an entirely destitute condition.

Another colony from Germany of several thousand persons were induced to leave their homes and embark for the fancied paradise to be found in Louisiana. They sailed in 1716 or 1717, under the leadership of the notorious John Law, who instead of bringing them immediately on their arrival in America to the promised Eden, landed them at the swamps near Mobile. Here they were exposed, without protection against many foes for five years. Not one of them entered the promised paradise. Two thousand were consigned to the grave, and only about three hundred of the survivors reached the banks of the Mississippi river in 1722. [Prof. Rupp.]

The brief notes that we have of the trials of these refugees, remind us constantly of Longfellow's Acadians.

"Far asunder on separate coasts, the Acadians landed;
Friendless, homeless, hopeless, they wandered from city to city,"
From the cold lakes of the North, to the sultry Southern savanna.

We have given these incidents in order to show the trials and sufferings endured by the people who composed the first congregations of the German Reformed Church in this country. Like the Pilgrim fathers at Plymouth, they came to brave the dangers of the wilderness, because of religious persecution. They brought their German Bibles and hymn-books with them, and a clergyman always accompanied them when they came in large bodies.

Yet it is not claimed for them that they were always in the right, and that their opponents were always intentionally unjust. Many of their severe trials in America came from their poverty, and the fact that owing to their foreign language and customs, they were frequently misunderstood. Misfortune too may have made them somewhat stubborn in spirit, and troublesome to their English-speaking neighbors. It is not necessary to throw the mystery and charm of romance over their pitiable condition. They were befriended by the Hollanders and the English on many occasions, and were freely welcomed to the Province of Pennsylvania. Yet even here suspicions were aroused against them, when they came in such swarms to occupy the land, and they were generally pushed out upon the frontier to cope with the treacherous savages; and even there found difficulty in securing good titles to the farms they had cleared from the forest. Added to this misfortune, was the fact that many of them were bound out to service for a term of years, to pay for their passages across the ocean.

Mr. Weiss Organizes the Church in Philadelphia.

On September 21st, 1727, a sloop named "William and Sarah," containing four hundred of these German immigrants, anchored in the Delaware river, here at Philadelphia. The list of passengers, as registered by the government officials, is headed by the name George Michael Weiss, V. D. M—*i. e.*, minister of the Word of God. He was the first minister to effect an organization of the German Reformed Church in this city. We have no means of arriving at the exact date of the organization, but from the following documents it is evident that it could not have been earlier than 1727, when Mr. Weiss first landed, nor later than 1729, when he sailed again for Europe.

From evidence given before the Chancery Court of Pa., on Nov. 23, 1732, by seven responsible witnesses, we have the following: "The said deponents, under oath testify that a number of Germans or Palatines, had, some time before that, formed themselves into a religious congregation in Philadelphia, where they resided, under the care of George Michael Weiss, a Protestant minister of the Reformed Religion, and a native of Germany, and are known by the name of the German Reformed Church in Philadelphia." This proves that Mr. Weiss organized this congregation, before the date of the deposition—1732.

We have also an old letter from the Rev. Mr. Andrews, Presbyterian minister of this city, dated August 14, 1730, bearing on the same subject, found in Hazzard's Register, vol. xv., p. 198. He writes: "There is in this province, a vast number of Palatines, and they come in still every year. Those that have come of late years are mostly Presbyterians, or as they call themselves, Reformed. They did use to come to me for baptism, and many have joined with us in the other sacrament. They never had a minister till about nine years ago, who is a bright young man, and a fine scholar. He is at present absent, being gone to Holland, to get money to build a church in this city." This confirms the fact stated in the deposition, that Mr. Weiss, the young minister referred to here, organized the congregation; but Mr. Andrews seems to have been under a mistake in stating that Mr. Weiss had been here nine years in 1730; the fact, as we have seen, is that he landed here in 1727.

We have, besides these papers, another bearing on this point, published as a notice in the Philadelphia Mercury, Feb. 3, 1729:

"This is to give notice, that the subscriber hereof, being desirous to be as generally useful as he can in this country, (wherein he is a stranger), declares his willingness to teach Logic, Natural Philosophy, Metaphysics, &c., to all such as are willing to learn. The place of teaching will be at the Widow Sprogel's on Second street, where he will attend, if he has encouragement, three times a week, for that exercise."

Signed by G. M.,
Minister of the Reformed Palatine Church.

From this it appears that Mr. Weiss lived here in the early part of the year 1729, and though he organized a congregation named Skippach, 24 miles out of the city, at about the same time, he must have preached here until he sailed for Europe, to collect books and funds for the mission churches. As he sailed in this same year, 1729, we fix the organization here at the year 1728.

The Ministry of Mr. Boehm.

His successor in this congregation was the Rev. John Philip Boehm, who arrived in this country about 1726, and settled in Whitpain Township, Montgomery County, where a Reformed Church, bearing his name, is now located. When he began his ministry here this congregation had no church-building, but worshiped in a building owned by one Wm. Allen. Mr. Schlatter's Church Journal, still in our possession, gives the following: "From November, 1734, the congregation had worshiped in an old, small, frame house, alternating each Sabbath with the Lutheran congregation. But after the Evangelicals (*i. e.* Lutherans,) had built their stone church in 1744, the Reformed worshiped alone, and paid Wm. Allen the sum of £4 yearly, for the above named church-house in Arch street, adjacent to the Quaker burial ground." Here Mr. Boehm preached one Sabbath in each month in this old, small frame building, on Arch street, which tradition reports to have been originally a barn.

Mr. Boehm seems to have been a man of untiring energy, as well as of good abilities. He soon set about the work of securing a lot for the location of a new church building, and finally fixed upon the spot where we are now worshiping. It was purchased for the congregation, by one Peter Wager, on March 12, 1741, and contained 49½ feet on Sassafras (now Race) street, by 204 feet in depth, being the Westerly side of our present church grounds. On the 18th of June following, Mr. Boehm, in connection with the Elder, Jacob Siegel, purchased the lot now contained in the N. E. corner of Franklin Square, of John Penn, Proprietary, in trust for, and for the use of the German congregation in Philadelphia, as a burying-ground. The price paid was £50; and five shillings yearly as quit-rent.

About this time, Mr. Boehm was involved in an unpleasant controversy with Count

Zinzendorf, the founder of the Moravian Church, in this country, growing out of the fact of the joint occupation of the Wm. Allen house, by the Reformed and Lutherans. Many of the Lutherans desired to have the Count for a Pastor, but Mr. Boehm was regarded as unfavorable to the arrangement, though he disclaimed any intention of speaking for any one but his own people. The Count withdrew, in 1742, with 34 of his adherents, and formed the First Moravian congregation, on Race street below Third street. The spirit of controversy subsisting between the two ministers, appears never to have spread through their respective congregations, for they dwelt here on Race street, as near neighbors for many years subsequently, with apparent harmony and friendship.

Mr. Schlatter installed as Pastor.

Mr. Boehm continued to supply the congregation until the arrival of Rev. Michael Schlatter,[*] from St. Gall, Switzer-

---
[*] In his Journal he writes his name SLATTER; evidently intending this orthography for English readers; but we have here followed the original Swiss form in order to avoid confusion.

land, who reached Philadelphia Sept. 6th, 1746, who then took charge of the church here. He was sent, at his own request, by the Deputies of the Synod of South and North Holland; and received instructions from them, to visit the various German Reformed congregations in the provinces, to organize new charges, and to invite the different German ministers already in the field, to organize themselves into a Coetus. And with all this, he was at the same time to serve in a charge as regular pastor. Mr. Schlatter was installed upon call of the congregation, by Mr. Boehm, on Jan. 1st, 1747, as regular pastor of the Philadelphia Reformed Church. And it is to his lasting honor, that he refused to receive any salary for the first year, "in order," as he said, "that by deed I might convince them that I did not serve them merely for the sake of my bread." The congregation then numbered about 100 members. The Germantown congregation was constituted a part of the Philadelphia charge, and the installation took place there on Feb. 15th, following.

The new pastor took pains to prepare church records, to which we are indebted for many facts in our early history. The record, now in our possession, commences on April 6th, 1747, giving the names of pastor and consistory. One item of business transacted was as follows: "Action was taken to remit a debt of £4, due the church from Mr. John Bürger, School-master and Chorister," showing that they had already, a parochial school. Another meeting was held April 12, to provide money for house rent; and another on Oct. 1st, immediately after which, the pastor went to New York on an interesting errand, already foreshadowed in the provision made for house rent. He was married to Maria Henrica Schleidorn, of New York, Oct. 11th, 1747. The newly married couple were domiciled upon their return, in a house rented of Mr. Wm. Brentsen, just opposite the new church here on Race street.

The First Church Building.

Under the date of Dec. 6th, we find the following entry in the Church Journal: "On the Second Advent Sunday, St. Nicholas day, the writer Michael Schlatter, minister here, for the first time preached in the new six-cornered Reformed Church, in the Race place, on the words of David, in the 65th Psalm, 5th verse (4th in the English Bible). But the church was not yet plastered, and had neither gallery nor window." And yet in mid-winter the members of the congregation were worshiping there—how does this comport with our easy church-going ideas and practices? This church building must have been of very quaint appearance, as shown in our cut. It was a stone or brick structure, hexagonal in form, with a hipped-roof, sloping from each of the six sides to the cupola. The cupola was also hexagonal, with an arch-topped narrow window in each side. Surmounting this was a ball, pierced by a rod projecting to quite an elevation, with the figure of a cock (the usual Holland symbol), at the top, as a vane.*

---

* In Scull and Heap's map of Philadelphia, 1753-4, the cupola is shown as that of the "Dutch Calvinistic Church."

The Organization of the First Synod.

The Holland authorities had instructed Mr. Schlatter to prepare the way for the organization of a Coetus, or Synod. Accordingly, he invited Revs. Weiss, Bœhm, Reiger and Dorstius, the four regular Reformed ministers already in the field, to meet here in Philadelphia on October 12, 1746. The meeting was held at the time, and all were present, except Mr. Dorstius, who was unable to come—they had never before been together, though some of them had labored in the various settlements for some twenty years. They drew up "articles of peace," before adjourning, preliminary to the regular organization of a Coetus, or Synod. The full organization of the Synod— the first regular ecclesiastical body, higher than a consistory, of the German Reformed Church in this country—took place here also. On September 29th, 1747, thirty-one brethren, including elders, convened in Mr. Schlatter's house, across the way, from whence at 9 o'clock, A. M. they proceded to the church, where the Rev. J. B. Reiger opened the Synod with a sermon founded on the 133d Psalm. In the afternoon, at 2 o'clock, the first business session was commenced—all the sessions were "opened with prayer and closed with thanksgiving." The Second Annual Meeting was held here also the year following, on September 29th, 1748.

Controversy between Mr. Schlatter and Mr. Steiner.

Hitherto Mr. Schlatter had met with apparently good success in his congregation, but the year following, in Sept., 1749, a minister named John Conrad Steiner, from Europe, arrived in Philadelphia, with credentials from the Holland Church. He was destined to be a rival to Mr. Schlatter, and as affairs turned out was a source of great trouble to him. Mr. Schlatter, by virtue of his prominent position, had recommended Mr. Steiner to the Reformed congregation at Lancaster, who gave him a call without having heard him or consulted with him. At first Mr. Steiner expressed himself as willing to go, but on account of sickness in his family, was detained for a time; when it transpired that a certain part of this congregation desired to have him as their pastor in the place of Mr. Schlatter. Mr. Steiner seems to have allowed the matter to be agitated, and for this has been very highly censured by later writers. The matter came to be decided by vote, and there was found to be a majority in favor of Mr. Steiner, both here and in Germantown. A controversy ensued, as to which party should have possession of the church; and Mr. Schlatter at one time concluded to leave, and entered the pulpit for the purpose of preaching his farewell sermon, but his feelings overcame him, and reading Matt. x. 14, he left the church. On Jan. 14, 1750, Mr. Steiner and his friends attempted to hold service in the church, when Mr. Schlatter and his friends were present, when some disputing followed, and finally both parties adjourned, leaving the key with the civil authorities. Finally a committee was chosen jointly by the two parties, and the whole matter referred to them, and they reported in favor of Mr. Schlatter.

The First Rival Congregation.

This ended the present troubles, and the Steiner party removed; and, according to Prof. Kalm and Mr. Ritter, they erected a new church building on Race street, below Third street. Prof. Kalm, who was here at that time, writes as follows: "The new Reformed Church was built at a little distance from the old one by the party of the clergyman who had lost his cause. This man however had influence enough to bring over to his party almost the whole audience of his antagonist, at the end of the year 1750, and therefore this new church will soon be useless." Mr. Ritter, in his history of the Moravian Church, says: "This building (Steiner's Church?) was about forty feet square, two and a half stories high, and supposed to be the first German Reformed Church in this city. It was purchased and altered into two dwellings by Mr. Ball. Philip Wager, the elder, occupied the one as a bakery; but Mr. John R. Baker and Godfrey Haga afterwards purchased the property and raised it to three stories, as it now stands (1857), and lived in it." Mr. Steiner remained with the opposition congregation here for only about two years, when, for lack of pecuniary support, he withdrew and served the congregation at Germantown for some three years longer.

In 1751 Mr. Schlatter returned to Europe to solicit funds, and if possible to bring ministers to supply the growing interests of the Germans in this vicinity. He returned with money, and also brought six young men who were ordained in Holland for the ministry. Upon his return here Mr. Schlatter entered upon his pastoral labors again, but the friends of Mr. Steiner did not reunite in the old church-work. Finally they called Rev. John Caspar Rübel to be the successor of Mr. Steiner—he was one of the young men who came with Mr. Schlatter—whether this settlement was with the advice and consent of the latter is not known. Both congregations were weak in their separated condition, and, as might be expected, no great prosperity was enjoyed by either. At last, in 1755, the matter was brought to the attention of the Synod, and an attempt was made for union and reconciliation. An article of agreement was drawn up between Mr. Schlatter and Mr. Rübel requiring them both to resign and vacate their charges, which both signed. They preached their farewell sermons on April 27, 1755. It was supposed that the two congregations here would now unite and call some minister who had no record in the case of their past troubles.

It would be interesting, if time permitted, to follow the record of Mr. Schlatter's life further, as he now takes leave of this, his beloved congregation. But time forbids— one incident only must here suffice. When, in September, 1777, during the Revolutionary war, the British invaded Germantown, Mr. Schlatter (who had before this been a chaplain in the American army, when the conflict took place at Nova Scotia against the French,) was residing at Chestnut Hill. He was ordered to assume his duties as chaplain in the British army—he refused, because he sided with the colonists; was arrested, and was immediately taken to Philadelphia and imprisoned. His house on Chestnut Hill was entered and plundered by British soldiers. They broke his furniture, threw his silver-ware into the well, and put his papers upon a pile and consumed them. How long he was confined in prison is not known; it was not however for a long time. But during the remainder of the war he was loyal to the American cause, and his sons served in our army. He died at Chestnut Hill in the Autumn of 1790, in the 75th year of his age. His ashes lie in the old Reformed graveyard in Franklin Square.

The Synod recommended to the united congregation here, after the resignation of Revs. Schlatter and Rübel, that they secure the Rev. Wm. Stoy (one of the six young men who came with Mr. Schlatter) as a supply. He was anxious to remain as their regular pastor, but was not acceptable to them, and removed in a little over one year.

The Ministry of Mr. Steiner.

In 1759 the united congregation, much

to the surprise and displeasure of the members of Synod, who were not consulted, called for their pastor the Rev. John Conrad Steiner, the former rival of Mr. Schlatter. He began his work here on May 20th of that year, and continued it with great acceptance and popularity until his death, which occurred some three years later. We have an old Mss. of his, among the archives, giving in full the articles of school regulation of great interest. He also published a volume of sermons on the Second Coming of Christ, marked with vigor of thought and ability. He died on July 6th, 1762, aged 55 years, 6 months, and 6 days. His ashes also repose in the old Burying-ground at Franklin Square.

Ancient School Regulations.

The following is a translation of the School Regulations, drawn up by Mr. Steiner, about the year 1760, for the government of the Race street Parochial School, for which the congregation had erected a building in 1753-4. We have given this document in full, and with care as to its translation, in order that the spirit of the German Parochial School System, may be better understood by us English-speaking people. The contrast between the warm Christian sentiment embodied in nearly all these articles, and our falsely negative position on Bible reading in the public schools, must be apparent to all readers.

"*School Regulations of the Reformed Congregation in Philadelphia.*" When well organized Christian congregations, for their upbuilding, establish schools, it is very important to have competent God-fearing men for teachers, that becoming order and propriety may be observed. On this account the Elders and Deacons of the Reformed Church in Philadelphia, unanimously agree to do all in their power for the welfare of such a well-regulated school, and for the upbuilding of our congregation, that all things may be done decently and in order. The following article is made, respecting the duty of the teacher, and the amount of salary he is to receive. He must be possessed of the following accomplishments:

First. He must be qualified in reading, writing, arithmetic and singing—he must undergo an examination in these branches and be approved.

Second. He must be one that takes a lively interest in, and helps to build up the Christian church; and must be also a God fearing virtuous man, and lead an exemplary life and must himself be a lover of the Word of God, and be diligent in its use as much as possible, among the children in school; and he must set a good example, especially before the young children. and avoid exhibitions of anger.

Third. He shall willingly and heartily seek to fulfill the duties obligatory upon him, with love to God and to the children; to the performance of which, the Lord their Maker, and Jesus their Redeemer, have so strongly bound him.

The following are the *Duties* incumbent upon the school-master.

First. He is not to show partiality among

the children, and he must receive them lovingly and without distinction.

Second. He must teach six hours per day—three in the forenoon, and three in the afternoon—unless the number of the scholars increases, when he must give them more time.

Third. He must be judicious, and adapt himself to the various dispositions, and gifts of the children; and exercise patience, love, and gentleness, as much as possible, in his teaching, that he may win their hearts, and work with blessing among them.

Fourth. He shall have power to correct and punish the children, though with moderation and forbearance, without animosity, or passion, or anger; and in particular he shall not treat them in a spiteful manner, but should rather consider the weakness of the children; and more particularly still he must refrain from all vexatious, abusive, and disgraceful language.

Fifth. He shall at all times open and close his school with a hearty prayer to God for His grace and blessing.

Sixth. Besides teaching the children to read and write, he shall also train them to pray, and exhort them to continue the practice. And besides teaching them the Lord's Prayer (Our Father, &c.), he shall also teach them the articles of our Christian faith, the Ten Commandments, and several short, edifying, penitent prayers, as well as scriptural passages—which he must repeat to them and impress upon their attention. They must also be taught to live a Godly life; to remember their Saviour, and to be obedient to their parents, and to conduct themselves in a becoming manner, especially in receiving proper admonition.

Seventh. If it is possible, and time will permit, he should sing several verses with the larger children, of pieces with which they are acquainted, and continue the practice from time to time, in order to instruct them in the art of singing.

Eighth. All those children who are able to read shall diligently learn the Catechism by heart; and this shall be strictly followed up until they are able to recite all the questions and answers. And finally, he shall look upon the Pastor of the congregation as the principal superintendent of the school, and acknowledge him as such. All complaints against the teacher, if any arise, shall be brought before the minister, and be subjected to his advice and counsel; who shall at all times be dignified, honorable and trustworthy, living in peace and friendship, as an elder and member in common with all his brethren; so that God's kingdom may be planted more and more among the old and young, and the kingdom of Satan be obstructed and destroyed.

Besides the above-mentioned school rules, the school-master obligates himself, in the absence of the minister, or in case of his sickness or inability to preach, that he will read some verses of Scripture, &c., to the edification of the congregation. He shall also be the foresinger (precentor, or chorister) and organist, and during the services all is committed unto him.

For the faithful performance of the foregoing duties, he shall receive a stipulated salary.

First. Each child shall pay five shillings per quarter for tuition. But in case the parents are poor, the Elders may pay the teacher three shillings out of the church treasury.

Second. The teacher has a right to all parts of the school-house at his pleasure; with the understanding, however, that the upper room be reserved for the use of the congregation, in case they need the same.

Third. The congregation shall pay the teacher a yearly salary of £8. The teacher hereby binds himself with his own handwriting and signature that he will, by the grace of God, fulfill these duties now made obligatory upon him."

The Ministry and Fall of Mr. Rothenbühler.

The next minister who served this charge was the Rev. Frederick Rothenbühler. He was originally from Switzerland, but at the time that he was called to the pastorate of this charge, July 30th, 1762, was settled in New York. His call provided for his preaching in the morning and afternoon on each Sabbath, and for a lecture from him each Thursday evening. He was to administer the Sacraments, visit the sick, catechise the youth, "and by all his acts and conversation to conduct himself as it becometh a true servant of Jesus Christ." In this last particular, however, he failed, for it seems that he was intemperate. The Consistory, as soon as they had proof of his guilt, cited him before them, and as he resented their admonitions, they called the leading members of the congregation together, and resolved to dismiss him. Mr. Rothenbühler had a few friends who sustained him, and he appealed to the Synod, as did also the Consistory. The Synod met on May 6, 1763, and resolved to sustain the Consistory, on condition, that they give them a pledge and bond, that they would, as a congregation, forever remain in union with the Synod. This bond was duly executed.

The Second Rival Congregation.

Mr. Rothenbühler, with his friends, then organized an independent congregation, which they named St. George's, and in 1763 took up a lot on Fourth Street below New Street, with a view of erecting a church building. The building was to be fifty-five by eighty-five feet in size. Its cost far exceeded their calculations, and the persons who became responsible for the amount expended were finally thrown into the debtors' prison. When their acquaintances inquired of them, as they looked through the prison windows, "For what were you put in jail?" they replied, "For building a church." To go to jail for building a church became a proverb in the City of Brotherly Love.

Their building was sold June 12th, 1770, to one Mr. Hockley, for £700, and two days afterward was transferred by him to Miles Pennington, a Methodist, for £500, in which connection it still remains, and is now known as St. George's M. E. Church on Fourth Street, and is said to be the oldest organization of that denomination in the city. Mr. Rothenbühler died with fever, and was buried in Franklin Square, August 9th, 1766, and his congregation disbanded and separated.

After the dismissal of Mr. Rothenbühler from this church, the Consistory held a correspondence with Rev. Wm. Otterbein, with a view to calling him. The correspondence lasted from May till September, 1763, but as Mr. Otterbein was slow in reaching a conclusion, it was dropped. Mr. Otterbein's letters are still in our possession.

Dr. Weyberg Installed as Pastor.

The choice of the congregation now fell upon a most worthy and eminent minister of the Reformed Church, Rev. Caspar Dietrich Weyberg, D. D., who was then settled at Easton, Pa. He was a Swiss by birth, educated in Europe, and came to this country about the year 1762. He accepted the call to become pastor of this congregation, and entered upon his duties November 13, 1763. Many are the evidences of the faithfulness and success of his long pastorate here. The church now enters upon a long period of peace and prosperity, a happy contrast to the times of trouble already experienced. He found about two hundred heads of families belonging to the old congregation, and proceeded to visit and catechize the youth, and gather in many to the communion of the church.

The Charter and Second Church Building.

On September 25, 1765, the charter for the congregation was obtained from John Penn, a descendant of the original William, under which we are still acting. The affairs of the church were now tending to great prosperity, under Dr. Weyberg's fruitful ministry; and it soon became apparent that the old Hexagon Church-building was too small for the constantly increasing audiences. Accordingly a movement was undertaken for a new and more commodious house of worship. The lot lying on the east side of the old church had been purchased of Richard Hill and others, on June 26th, 1749, some twenty years previously, containing 60 feet on Race street by 138 in depth—this gave them all the ground out to Sterling alley (Hillsdale street), with a frontage on Race street of 109½ feet. At a congregational meeting, held on August 19th, 1771, it was resolved that the new building should stand east and west, and be 90 feet in length by 65 feet in width. In 1772 the collection of money began, and in the following year an appeal for aid was forwarded to the old mother church in the Palatinate. A copy of this document is still in our possession. The foundation stone was laid April 10th, 1772, and the corner-stone on the 28th of the same month, both with religious services. And on May 1st, 1774, the new church was dedicated, in the presence of the Governor of the State, English and Lutheran ministers, and a large assembly of people.

Revolutionary Incidents.

And now the clouds of war began to gather, foretokening the Revolutionary struggle. Dr. Weyberg from the first was a strong friend of the Colonists, and he took no pains to conceal his sentiments. And when the British troops entered this city, September, 1777, and began what is known as the "Occupation," a son of Weyberg's, who stood in the door of his father's house, shouted as the troops were passing: "Hurrah for General Washington!" To which the soldiers replied, in muttered tones: "You rebel!" Dr. Weyberg took a decided stand in favor of the patriotic efforts which were made by his countrymen to assert their independence. During the "Occupation" he preached to the Hessians, who thronged to hear him in great crowds. He boldly asserted the justice of the American cause, and bore down upon the wickedness of their oppressors with such energy that the British began to feel the effects of his fearless appeals in the daily desertion of their Hessian mercenaries. In order to put a stop to his preaching they threatened his life, and threw him into prison. He was, however, soon liberated." Dr. Berg (from whom the above statements are quoted) adds: "I have been assured by aged members of the church that it used to be confidently affirmed that the Hessians would in all probability, to a man, have left the British service if the old father had not been silenced."

On September 26th, 1777, during the time of Dr. Weyberg's imprisonment, the British occupied his new church as a hospital, and greatly injured and defaced it. On May 5th, 1779, he wrote to the Classis of Amsterdam thus: " Whilst the British had this town in possession my congregation was scattered, my beautiful church was torn up, and converted into a hospital. To the members who still remain here I preach in the school-house. At the present time, the people are returning again, and take possession of their dwellings; still, many, from fear of the British, remain in the country. On the other hand, however, many strangers have moved into the city, so that my congregation is as strong again as it was before." The first sermon he preached, after having been liberated, was from the text, Ps. 79 : 1 : "O God! the heathen are come into thine inheritance: Thy holy temple have they defiled." Harbaugh, Lives of the Fathers, Vol. II., p. 103. Of such stern stuff our Revolutionary fathers were made—nothing seemed to dampen their enthusiasm, nor subdue their courage. The cost of repairing the church after the British vacated it was $15,200.

After this, Dr. Weyberg went on with his ministry here with that calm determination that was characteristic of his whole life. He was accustomed to preach the truth with great plainness to his congregation, and often, in reproving his people for the wickedness of their children, would say: "The apple does not fall far from the tree." He is described as having been a tall, slim man, with a powerful voice, always carrying his Bible under his arm when on his way to church.

The affection with which Dr. Weyberg was regarded by his people, may be known by the sentiment of the following hymn, composed and sang upon the occasion of his funeral:

> " These hearts, O God, are rent with grief,
> Our eyes are filled with tears—
> Thy mourning people now bereft
> Of him they loved, must fly to Thee!
> O Lord! our pastor is no more!
> Sealed are those lips, which once
> Bade sinners turn and live—
> Weyberg, who meekly bore his cross,
> And gloried in the shame, and did not shrink
> From duty when it brought distress—
> Ah! he has left us never to return.
>
> * * * * * * * *
>
> Father, farewell! Thy crown be bright
> Until we meet in realms of light."
>
> *Translated by Dr. Berg.*

He died on August 21st, 1790, having served this congregation most acceptably for twenty-six years. His remains were also buried in Franklin Square.

The Rev. Mr. Winkhaus Installed as Pastor.

The Race street congregation called for their next pastor the Rev. John Herman Winkhaus, originally from Germany, but at the time, pastor of the Reformed Church at the Trappe, Montgomery County, Pa. He preached his introductory sermon here on Sept. 26th, 1790. His pastorate was short, though not without good fruits and prosperity. He died on Oct, 3d, 1793, in his 35th year, of yellow fever, which prevailed during that season so fearfully and fatally. He contracted his sickness while visiting Mr. Schreiner, the School-master, who subsequently, also, died of the contagion. He thus fell at his post of duty. His remains lie in Franklin Square, beside the other pastors.

Dr. Hendel Succeeds to the Pastorate.

His successor was the Rev. William Hendel, D.D., who was a native of the Palatinate, but had preached in this country for some years, (like the others), and was far advanced in life when he began his ministry here on Feb. 9th, 1794. He too is a man of Revolutionary honors. During the war, he frequently visited a new congregation in the Lykens Valley, and was guarded by armed men, when going to the place where he was to preach—the guards standing at the door, with their arms to defend him from the Indians, and accompanying him upon his return homeward. Dr. Hendel was a father whose memory is very precious in the Reformed Church. He is described by Dr. Harbaugh, as having been very venerable and saintly in appearance. When he ministered here, it is said; "that his hair was long and white, his countenance serene and heavenly, and his whole appearance beautifully venerable and saintlike. He could scarcely hold the hymn-book in his trembling hands." He is called the St. John of the Reformed Church. And any one who glances at his hand-writing in our records, will see that he was exceedingly tremulous. But while his natural force was somewhat abated, his courage was by no means gone.

Second Pestilence of Yellow Fever.

A second time the pestilence of the yellow fever swept over the city, and Dr. Hendel, faithful to his post as a minister of Christ to the sick and dying, at last fell, a victim to the deadly contagion. I cannot forbear quoting the words of Dr. Berg, spoken in this house in 1839. He says: "Some of you, my hearers, well remember that season of panic and dismay, when our city was, for a time, converted into a Golgotha. You remember the almost deserted streets, the fearful silence, which told you that the pestilence was spreading its broad, dark wings over the habitation of men. You can recall the hurried preparation for the funeral. . . Men of stout hearts were afraid to meet the coffins that were to be seen in every street, lest the deadly contagion might point its arrow next at them. Most of the pastors of the churches had left their people, and nearly all the wealthy inhabitants had deserted the city."

. . . . When this second visit of the pestilence came, Dr. Hendel did not desert his post. He was with the sick: his place was at the house of mourning. The blessing of those that were ready to perish came upon him, until he could visit no more, and then, he was soon gathered to his fathers." He died on Sept. 29th, 1798, smitten by the pestilence, and his ashes repose by the side of Steiner, Weyberg and Winkhaus, in Franklin Square.

What thoughts do not the mention of such names as Weyberg, Winkhaus, and Hendel, stir within us, as we review their acts that testify of their faith in God, their love to souls, and their steadfast continuance in the work of the ministry, even with the martyr spirit! But like St. Paul, these, too, have "fought their last fight"; they are long since gone to their heavenly reward. And as we stand here, watching these figures recede from our vision into the mighty past, as friends stand on the beach and look after vessels carrying their loved ones far from their sight over the mighty ocean, we can only repeat the lines of the pious Doddridge:

> "Our fathers, where are they,
> With all they called their own?
> Their joys and griefs, and hopes and cares,
> And wealth and honor gone!
>
> God of our fathers hear,
> Thou everlasting Friend!
> While we, as on life's utmost verge
> Our souls to Thee commend.
>
> Of all the pious dead
> May we the footsteps trace,
> Till with them, in the land of light,
> We dwell before Thy face."

PART II.

A HISTORY

OF THE

Reformed Church in Philadelphia,

Between the Years 1800 and 1876.

PSALM 48 : 12, 13.

"Walk about Zion, and go round about her; tell the towers thereof. Mark ye well her bulwarks, consider her palaces; that ye may tell it to the generation following."

State of the Congregation in 1800.

Before tracing the history of the Reformed Church in Philadelphia, into the present century, we would do well to pause and note the important features of the records already presented. We notice that up to this time, (about the year 1800), there has been but this one permanently established German Reformed congregation in the city. The attempts at organizing independent congregations made in 1750, and in 1763, were both failures.

Loyalty of Pastors and People.

We may also recall with just pride, the thorough loyalty of the pastors of this congregation, to the American cause in the days of the Revolution. The memory of Schlatter and Weyberg, may well be cherished by us as heroes among the Revolutionary fathers, who suffered the spoiling of their goods, and the imprisonment of their persons for their loyalty to the sacred cause of independence.

And that the members of this congregation sympathized with their pastors, in their loyalty to the American cause, is proved from the fact, that at least on two occasions they freely opened the doors of their church, for memorial services, rendered to distinguished officers of the American Army. The first occasion was upon the death of Major General Richard Montgomery, of

Revolutionary fame; who was killed on Dec. 31st, 1775, in the famous attack upon the city of Quebec. At a meeting held here, in the Second Church building, Dr. Weyberg, pastor, on Feb. 19th, 1776, Mr. William Smith, pronounced a Eulogy on General Montgomery. At that time the opinions of citizens here were very much divided, on the subject of the war, and no greater proof of their loyalty to the American cause could be given by pastor and people, than the opening of the doors of their new and highly prized house of worship, for this purpose.

The other occasion alluded to was a similar meeting held here upon the death of General Washington. The society of the Cincinnati, founded in 1783, by the officers of the Revolutionary army, of which General Washington, himself was the first President, met to commemorate the death of the fallen chieftain. The meeting was held in the same building, then standing on this consecrated place, on Feb. 22d, in the year 1800. It is only an act of justice on our part, to put on record here in this centennial year, the fact of the unswerving loyalty of the fathers in this church, to the cause of our country.

This century opens upon our history, with the church and school in most flourishing condition. The large church building erected here in 1772, in which these memorial services were held, then one of the most commodious in the city was filled from Sabbath to Sabbath, with devout worshipers. As this building is distinctly remembered by the older members of the congregation, and the citizens in the neighborhood, it may be interesting to give here, a brief description.

Description of the Second Church Building.

It is described as having been a large structure. It was 90 feet long, on Race street, with large double doors near either end, having at their tops a very heavy ornamental coping. A low brick wall, covered with flat stones, ran along the sidewalk in front, upon which was an iron railing or fence, with gates located at the few steps fronting either entrance. The building was of brick; with here and there a brick burned black and glazed, set in the wall by way of ornamentation, as is now seen in many of our older buildings still standing. Between the doors in front were two windows, with corresponding ones in the second story, for lighting the gallery. The East gable on Sterling alley, had two windows below, with a large central one in the second story, and a circular one in the attic. The width of the building was 65 feet, and its height 42 feet. In the rear were two doors corresponding to those in front, between which was located the high pulpit with its spiral staircase, and a sounding-board, projecting over the head of the speaker.

Directly opposite, in the front gallery, was the organ, where the choir were stationed to sing the German hymns and chorals. The ceiling was high and arched, the gallery broad and firmly set, and the pews above and below deeply seated in the old-fashioned style. No arrangements were made for heating the building until Jan. 28, 1788, when a vote was taken on the question, whether the congregation should purchase stoves or not. It resulted in 10 yeas and 4 nays. Accordingly, on the 29th December, of the same year, two stoves were bought and placed in position in the church. The entrance to the church and the school-house yards, was by Sterling alley, to which the Eastern wall of the church extended. The church-yard was shaded with trees, and the walks paved with brick; and was separated by a fence from the school-house yard, in which there was a well of water.

Origin of the Parochial and Sunday-Schools.

In connection with the subject of the Parochial school-building, it will be remembered that such a school known as the Charity or Free school, had been sustained almost from the date of our organization. The first building was erected in 1753-4, and was torn down to give place to the larger structure, still standing in the rear of this house, which was built in 1796, and to which Mr. Helffenstein refers in his description.

The united interests of the church and its parochial school, were remembered by the legacies of many of the fathers and mothers in the church, who died between the years of 1762 and 1800. It is by this means that the school has been sustained for so many years, for the improvement of the intellect and morals, and the culture of religious habit and devotion, in the children of the congregation and neighborhood.

As a matter of historical record it may be well also to mention the fact, that the Sunday-school of this church, was established on April 14th, 1806, and opened with 40 scholars. We learn this from the report of the committee, rendered to the Board of Corporation in the month of February, 1807.

Rev. Samuel Helffenstein, Jr., adds this description concerning the parochial schools, and the church and mission services. "At this time (about the year 1800), the services on Sabbath were held in the morning and afternoon, and the weekly lecture on Thursday evening. Besides, there was a weekly evening service in the Northern Liberties school-house, alternately supplied by the pastors of the Lutheran and Reformed churches. And there was also occasional service held, particularly during the holidays, in the Kensington school-house. Both these school-houses were supplied with a pulpit in a reserved part of the building; and were under the special control, and were the property of the two churches, the Reformed owning the one in Kensington. The parochial school-house, more immediately connected with the Race Street Church, is still standing in the rear of the church edifice. In this building the weekly lecture, the Sabbath-school and vestry meetings were held. In the earlier history of the church, the school-master and the sexton, resided in the spacious building referred to; the school-master, in connection with his own proper duties, performed also the duty of organist." There are many persons still living, who can recall the pleasant features of the parochial school, held in the old school-house here when father Bibighaus was for many years the school-master, and also foresinger in the church. Here, during his long pastorate, the Rev. Dr. Helffenstein, had many students under his private tuition, studying for the ministry—at least twenty-seven were thus educated. They were accustomed to sit under the pulpit, in the chancel, during the church services; and in many cases were received into the pastor's home as regular members of the family. This was, in that day, a substitute for the Theological Seminary.

A singular custom of stretching a chain across the street in front of the church during the time of service, in order that there might be no interruption from passing vehicles, was practiced at this time, and should not be passed over without notice. These were in general, the local features of church life here at the opening of the present century.

It is pleasant, in this connection, also, to note the fact that a fraternal spirit was at that time cherished between the members of this congregation, and the old German Lutheran Church, worshiping at Fourth and Cherry streets. When their building was destroyed by fire in December, 1794, our Consistory took action, inviting them to worship in the Reformed Church till theirs should be rebuilt. This invitation they accepted, and worshiped here for nearly two years. They acknowledged the courtesy by a vote of their council, passed Nov. 17, 1796, thanking the Reformed people for their kindness, and stating that their new church would be ready for occupation Nov. 20th. At the same time our congregation raised $500, in their aid, while engaged in the erection of their own new school-building, involving on their own account a heavy expense.

The influences, and changes that came with the life of the new Republic, were now to be experienced by the German-speaking citizens. The "*crown*" that had rested upon the old organ, since its construction, as an emblem of the royal power to which the Colonists were subject at the time the church was erected, was now by vote of consistory removed, and the emblem of the Republic, the "*Federal Eagle*," in Aug. 1790, was substituted in its place. And the spirit of the times pointed to still more important changes soon to follow.

The Pastorate of Dr. Helffenstein.

Rev. Samuel Helffenstein, D.D., the regular successor of Mr. Hendel, was elected as pastor here on January 14th, 1799, "with a promised salary of £300, and free house as parsonage." The house that he occupied, during his entire pastorate, communicated with the church-yard, but fronted on Fourth street, and is still standing. For some four years, all seems to have gone on well with the congregation and their new pastor, who ministered exclusively in the German language. But on April 2d, 1804, a resolution was passed by the Consistory appointing a congregational meeting for the 8th of May following, to test the sentiment of the people on the question of having occasional preaching in the English language.

Troubles in Changing to the English Language.

This was to be the beginning of many serious troubles in the congregation. Next to the love of our native land, we all cherish our native language. And as the German fathers had lost their inheritance in the Fatherland, they seemed to be the more tenacious of their mother-tongue. But the inexorable logic of events, compelled a decision, and so the vote was taken. The result was almost a tie, and owing to some defects in the mode of procedure the election was declared illegal.

The agitation respecting the change of language continued, and various petitions came before the Consistory, advocating a change. During the year 1805, the matter was brought to the attention of the Synod, requesting them to recommend that preaching in the English language be allowed on every third Sabbath, "for the benefit of those who do not understand the German."

On July 9th, 1805, a motion was offered before the Consistory as follows: "Resolved, that as the Board of Corporation of the Race Street Church, and in conformity to the wish of Synod, we will introduce the English language into our services, before the congregation shall be destroyed through strife." The vote was taken, resulting in a tie; Dr. Helffenstein, the pastor, voting in the negative. A proposition followed from the party wishing English services, for compromise; but all efforts for an amicable arrangement for the use of both languages seem to have failed.

The Party in Favor of English Withdraw.

In the following year, 1806, those who were heartily in favor of the English language withdrew, and organized themselves into a separate congregation. As no minister was at hand from the German Reformed connection, to serve them in the English language, they established themselves in Crown street in 1808, under the charge of Rev. James K. Burch, a minister of the

Presbyterian Church. They finally connected themselves with the Reformed (Dutch) Church, and erected the building now standing on the West side of Crown street, opening it for worship in 1810. Mr. Burch was followed in the ministry by Revs. Joseph Broadhead, Jno. Ludlow, G. R. Livingstone, Dr. Bethune and others. It is said, that ours was the first congregation in the German Reformed Church, that made the attempt to change from the German to the English language. However this may be, it is evident that it was a great trial, almost destroying the charge before it was fully accomplished.

Though matters were temporarily relieved by the departure of the English-speaking portion of the congregation in 1806, the question was by no means settled. As the years sped on, the good old German fathers in the church found their own children, with the rising generation generally, inclining toward the vernacular of the country in which they lived, and demanding that services be rendered in English.

At last in 1817, the question pressed itself upon the attention of the church in a new form. The leaders of the party favorable to the German, succeeded in electing members to the Board of Corporation, in sympathy with their views. And at the same time they came to the conclusion (whether justly or not we do not know), that the pastor, Mr. Helffenstein, was favorable to the side of those who were struggling to secure the introduction of the English. The result was (as stated by Mr. Helffenstein, Jr.), that they took summary action in the Board and dismissed him from the pastorate.

Mr. Helffenstein, Jr., continues: " He was accordingly notified that his services were no longer required. On the following Sabbath he went as usual to the church, but instead of ascending the pulpit, took his stand before the altar, and gave the congregation an account of what the corporation had done." This produced strong expressions of sympathy, with the pastor, on the part his friends in the congregation.

"The next Sabbath the doors of the church were closed by the corporation, and the congregation, with the pastor, met for some time in the school-house for divine service. In the meantime an appeal was taken by the pastor and congregation to the Supreme Court, before which the case was argued by the ablest counsel in the city on both sides. The result was a writ of mandamus, commanding the corporation to open the church, and give the pastor possession of the pulpit."

The Germans Withdraw.

"When Mr. Helffenstein entered his pulpit on the following Sabbath, the leader of the corporation arose and said: '*Come, my brethren, this is not our minister*,' when the whole party left the church. In this they followed bad advice, it is said given by their counsel-at-law, as it rendered it very difficult for them to return and regain their former position." It will be remembered that this is the narrative of a son of the pastor, who naturally must have looked at the matter from an interested standpoint.

It is indeed to be deplored, that churches are sometimes called upon to pass through such great difficulties, because the members and ministers cannot "see eye to eye and lift up the voice together." But the changing of language was a real difficulty, and, in the nature of the case, would lead to divergence, of view and sentiment, and perhaps to estrangement.

The result of the withdrawal of the Germans in 1817, was the organization of a new German Church, which has grown in strength and has sent out colonies, and is still extending its efficiency and influence. They first met and worshiped in Old Commissioners' Hall, on Third street, and organized under the name of Salem's Reformed Church, in Sept. 1817, with 67 members. They then called the Rev. Frederick William Van Der-Sloot, Dec. 29, 1818, under whose pastorate they erected the old church-building in St. John street, below Green, where, afterwards, Dr. Bibighaus, (previously school-master and chorister here), ministered with great faithfulness and acceptance for many years. In the year 1873, the Salem's congregation erected the fine structure at Fairmount avenue and Fourth street, where they now worship. Mr. Helffenstein, who is our chief authority for this part of our narrative, thus continues in the Reformed Church Monthly, June number, 1869: "After the two secessions stated, and the introduction of an alternate German and English service, the Race Street Church continued to move on for some years, with as much prosperity, internal and external, as could be expected under the circumstances. The Sabbath service was encouragingly attended, the weekly meetings often crowded, and many seasons of gracious refreshment unostentatiously enjoyed. A regular meeting for exhortation and prayer was kept up for many years, an hour before the morning and evening service of the Sabbath, conducted by pious laymen and others in connection with the church. At last, however, it was found out, that no church in the cities, dependent upon the native population, and cut off from increase from abroad, could well succeed with two languages in its service.

Mr. Finney Introduces English Exclusively.

"The attempt was made and succeeded in 1828, to introduce the English language to the entire exclusion of the German. In this connection the Rev. Charles G. Finney, with consent of the pastor, was invited to supply the pulpit for a time, in the afternoon and evening of the Sabbath. The result was, the church was disorganized; and the pastor, who had expended the strength of his more vigorous days, felt it his duty to resign a charge he had held so many years, and served through so many difficulties."

The Rev. Jacob Helffenstein, of Germantown, in explanation of the statement made here that the church was disorganized, through the preaching of the Rev. Mr. Finney, says, that the contrast between the preaching of the powerful revivalist, and the plain presentation of Gospel truth, by his father, who was then far advanced in years, brought about the difficulty.

Mr. Finney, in his autobiography lately published, makes the following references to his services here in 1828. "In Race street there was a large German Church, the pastor of which was a Mr. Helffenstein. The elders of the congregation, together with their pastor, requested me to occupy their pulpit. Their house was then, I think, the largest house of worship in the city. It was always crowded; and it was said, it seated 3,000 people, when the house was packed and the aisles were filled. There I preached statedly for many months."

The pastoral relation between Dr. Helffenstein and this church was formally dissolved on April 1st, 1830, but the old father, reluctant to leave the pastorate he had held for over thirty years, continued to perform ministerial acts in the charge, and held services for a time, with a few members favorable to him, in a room at the corner of Fourth and Vine streets. He finally removed to North Wales, Montgomery county, where he died Oct. 17th, 1866, aged 91 years and 6 months. It is pleasant to know that no ill feeling resulted from Father Helffenstein's removal. As late as the year 1852 or '53, he filled this pulpit upon invitation of the congregation.

The Old Grave-yard in Franklin Square.

It is necessary that a word of explanation should be given here respecting the old grave-yard in Franklin Square. The city had authorized the bringing of a suit against the congregation, to eject them from the premises, in order that the ground could be thrown into a public square. In February, 1801, the Counsel agreed to discontinue the suit, on condition that the congregation yield to the city all parts of the square not used for interments; that they accept a lease from the city for those parts of the square on which interments had been made, but for which they held no patent; "and that they do not erect buildings on the lot for which they have a patent, and length of possession shall be no bar to city rights."

It seems that the Council feared that the congregation was about to erect a church building on the lot, and they were anxious to prevent it. By signing this agreement, which was done in August following, the congregation lost possession of much ground that had been occupied from time to time, adjacent to the lines of their original patent. To compensate them for this, an Act was passed by the Legislature of Pa., the next February, granting them a burying-ground of lands belonging to the State at Seventeenth and Cherry streets.

As yet the congregation was left in possession of the land originally granted by John Penn, but in 1835 the City Council renewed the suit to wrest this consecrated place, with the graves of the former ministers and members, from them.*

The Common Council passed a resolution

---

*" Directly east of the sparkling jets, a few feet from the edge of the circular gravel walk, under the green sod, lie the Revs. Steiner and Winkhaus, and Drs. Weyberg and Hendel, the aged. Directly north of this spot, about midway between it and Vine street, lies Rev. Michael Schlatter; and around these leaders of the Lord's host, far and near—a silent congregation now!—sleep thousands of those to whom they once ministered the holy ordinances of the Church, and the precious instructions and consolations of the Gospel."—*Harbaugh's Life of Schlatter, p.* 357.

to offer them $50,000 for their claim, but the Select Council refused to concur in the offer.

The case was then referred to the judges of the Supreme Court for decision, who found a bill of indictment against the officers of the church for thus occupying a portion of a public square, and commanded them to remove grave-stones and fence, and pay the costs of court. The church officers could now do nothing but submit, and the grave-stones were laid flat upon the graves, and the whole covered with earth. Two years afterward, the Council remitted the court charges and granted the sum of $5000 to the congregation, on condition that they relinquish all claim to the lot. This was done, and the money thus obtained was used for the construction of the vaults in the present church lot. The plea made use of by the Council to justify their repeated prosecutions, was that this land was one of the five public squares originally reserved by William Penn for the city, and that his grandson, John Penn, had no right to dispose of it in the first place. All this illustrates the truth of that saying that "Corporations have no souls."

Mr. Sprole Installed as Pastor.

The regular successor of Dr. Helffenstein as pastor in this congregation was the Rev. William T. Sprole, a minister from the Presbyterian Church. He took charge on May 1st, 1832, preaching exclusively in the English language. He seems to have been a vigorous man, and earnest in his calling. The church began to recover from the troubles brought on by the change of language, and the records show a good degree of prosperity.

With this new spirit came the desire for a new and more modern house of worship, and a location where there would not be so great annoyance from noises in the street. The old church was accordingly removed, and the present structure erected (in 1837,) in a position on the church lot further removed from the sidewalk, on Race street, along which the broad side of the old church was located. Soon after the completion of this building, in 1837, Mr. Sprole retired from the pastorate—his last communion record is dated March 4th, 1837, which was Easter Sunday, the day on which this church was dedicated. His resignation was handed in and accepted on the 1st of July following.

Pastorate of Dr. Berg.

The regular successor of Mr. Sprole in the pastorate of this church, was the Rev. Joseph F. Berg, D.D., well known to most of the members of the present congregation. His long and eventful pastorate here, and the preciousness of his memory to many of our hearts, makes it fitting that we record here, a brief sketch of his life.

He was born in the year 1812, in Antigua, one of the West India Islands, where his father was located as a missionary. His parents were the Rev. Christian Frederick, and Hannah Berg, members of the Moravian Church, in connection with which he also was reared, and received his literary and theological training. His early education was pursued in the Moravian schools in England. In 1825, he came to this country and continued his studies at the Moravian school at Nazareth, Pennsylvania. After completing the same, he remained in that institution a few years as Professor of Chemistry. In 1836, having received a call from the German Reformed Church in Harrisburg, Pa., he appeared before Synod, and requested to be received into its connection. His application being sustained, he was received, and, on the evening of Oct. 2d, was ordained and set apart to the work of the ministry. He remained at Harrisburg only a short time, when, being appointed to a professorship in Marshall College, he removed to Mercersburg, Pa. He remained there for only about one year, accepting the call to this church, and entering upon his duties here on Nov. 19th, 1837.

Prosperity of the Church.

The peculiar gifts of Dr. Berg, and his warm-hearted preaching and sociability among the people, were soon appreciated. At that time the whole district of the city, in the vicinity of the church, was filled with private residences. The new church-building was soon filled, so much so, that the pastor in recording the communion of Sept. 9th, 1838, wrote: "Hundreds crowded to their places at the feast, and the Lord was known of us in the breaking of bread."

On Sept. 29th, 1839, while the General Synod of the Reformed Church was in session here, the pastor preached a historical sermon entitled, "Christian Landmarks," afterward published in a small volume. In February, of the following year, mention is made of the fact that 32 persons were added to the church, and it is added "the revival is still in progress." This last expression refers to the great ingatherings that took place here, in this and subsequent years, in connection with protracted meetings, which brought vast concourses of people together, and gave prominence to both church and pastor. In the same year eighteen members of the Crown Street

Reformed (Dutch) Church came in a body, bringing regular letters of dismission, and united here.

Public Debates.

It was during this period that Dr. Berg held an argument before the public, with a Mr. Barker, who challenged the ministry of this city to meet him in defence of the truth of Christianity; against which he pretended to be arrayed, both in intellect and feeling. Many of the ministers here urged Dr. Berg to accept the challenge, which he finally did, and met the man, and in the opinion of persons qualified to judge of the arguments, vanquished the self-appointed champion of infidelity. Mr. Barker was subsequently converted to the Christian religion, and is said, to have died with confession of earnest faith in all its promises.

Dr. Berg also delivered a series of lectures here between the years 1840 and 1844, in opposition to Roman Catholicism, which drew together vast crowds of auditors. And many a sharp thrust did he give this "man of sin," as he was accustomed to call it, which added not a little to his reputation as a polemical speaker.

Dr. Berg's Farewell.

But it will be impossible for us to linger upon the details of Dr. Berg's pastorate longer; we must pass to its closing scene. In the year 1852, he handed his resignation to the Board of Corporation, and it was accepted. His farewell sermon, which was preached on the evening of March 14th, was subsequently printed, and from it we gain the following particulars.

In his introduction he says: "I do not relinquish this pulpit, which I have occupied for nearly fifteen years, because I have felt unable to maintain my position among you; it is not because you have, as a congregation, become alienated from my affections, that I come, this evening, to offer my last words of counsel as your pastor, and to make the last record of my ministry among you. As a congregation, in my official and in my private relations, you have made my abode with you pleasant and happy. . . . .

This hour is one to which I have looked forward as an ordeal of no ordinary intensity. It is a very sore trial to sunder the ties which have bound me to you for the last fifteen years. Yes, I avow it; this place is dear, very dear, to me."

It is generally known that Dr. Berg had, during his ministry here, become involved in an unpleasant controversy, with Rev. Dr. John W. Nevin, now for many years professor in one of the church's institutions, on the doctrinal issues underlying the subject of Liturgical worship. This was the commencement of the long controversy that has agitated the Reformed Church, even to the present time.

To this he makes allusion in the following paragraphs: "It is not because I have embraced doctrines adverse to the standards of the German Reformed Church, that I leave my ministerial associates and my ecclesiastical home."

Referring to the teachings of his opponent, he says: "You know that I protested against them in their incipiency. And I remember with gratitude the cordiality with which this congregation sustained me, when I stood in the painful position of recording my vote in solitary opposition, without a single voting ministerial associate to keep me in countenance against the overwhelming odds by which the new doctrines were sustained."

Toward the conclusion of the sermon he says: "Should any who hear me wish to know where an old friend may be found, if they will look for me in the Gibraltar of Protestantism, the old church of Holland, which has always been true to her history, and firm as a rock in support of the principles of the Reformation, I hope, if God permit, to find rest in her communion."

The intimation given in this paragraph was carried out by his entering the ministry of the Reformed Protestant (Dutch) Church. Some years before this a congregation was organized in this city known as the Second Reformed Dutch Church (under the pastorate of the Rev. Dr. Jacob C. Sears from 1825 to 1833), which, after various trials and discouragements, was compelled to give up its church edifice and suspend its services. There was, however, a fund left from this enterprise amounting to several thousand dollars, reserved for the use of the congregation in case of the renewal of their work. Dr. Berg availed himself of this advantage, and revived the organization, thus securing the fund. Quite a number of the members of this congregation followed him; and the movement resulted in the reorganization of the Second Reformed (Dutch) congregation, and the erection of the church edifice on Seventh street, above Brown, where the congregation still worships.

In 1861, Dr. Berg was elected by the General Synod of his church to the position of Professor of Didactic and Polemic Theology in the Theological Seminary at New Brunswick, N. J.; which position he accepted and held until the time of his death, which occurred on July 20th, 1871. It is pleasant to record here, as in the case of Dr. Helffenstein, that Dr. Berg returned to this charge, where he held a tender and life-long attachment, and ministered to the congregation as a supply during the greater part of the year 1870. Thus, in the evening of his days, as it were under the mellowing tints of life's sunset, he came back to his old church, and friends, to tell, as he was wont to do—

> "With earnest tones, and grave,
> The old, old story,
> Of unseen things above,
> Of Jesus and His glory,
> Of Jesus and His love."

The Ministry of Rev. Mr. Reid.

The Rev. Samuel H. Reid succeeded Dr. Berg, as regular pastor of this congregation, on October 1st, 1852. He served the charge acceptably, and received a number of new members, but could not be induced to remain for any great length of time. He retired from the pastorate August 31st, 1854.

Dr. Bomberger Installed as Pastor.

He was succeeded by the Rev. J. H. A. Bomberger, D. D., on September 1st of the same year. The incidents of his long pastorate here are fresh in the memory of nearly all the members of this church. The increase of the congregation under his ministry was uniformly encouraging; and in 1860, when he preached an anniversary sermon (afterwards published under the title of "*Five Years at the Old Race Street Church*"), he reported that 211 members had been added to the communion under his ministry.

The Tercentenary Convention.

An event of importance transpired here during Dr. Bomberger's pastorate, that is deserving of special mention in this history.

The Synods of the German Reformed Church had been for some time looking forward to, and making preparation for, the celebration of the three hundredth anniversary of the publication of the Heidelberg Catechism. This honored confession of faith, the doctrinal standard of the Reformed Church, was first sent forth, by Frederic III., Elector of the Palatinate, on January 19th, 1563, and it was therefore resolved to commemorate this event by a Tercentenary Convention. The Convention was appointed to meet in this church, and assembled here on Jan. 17th, 1863. It was a large and interesting assembly, and was handsomely entertained by this congregation, under the direction of its energetic pastor. "The church had been beautifully decorated with laurel wreaths and festoons, and presented quite a holiday aspect. On one side of the pulpit, encircled with a laurel wreath, was the date '1563,' and on the other, '1863,' decorated in like style." The sessions continued for nearly one week, during which time, essays and addresses were read and delivered, which have since been published in a large volume named "Tercentenary Monument." The whole occasion marked an epoch in the history of this branch of the Reformed Church, and is therefore worthy of special mention, even in this brief history.

Dr. Bomberger retired from the pastorate of this charge on April 1st, 1870, having accepted the Presidency of Ursinus College, an institution then just organized, over the growing success of which he still presides, "his bow abiding in strength, and the arms of his hands made strong by the hands of the Mighty God of Jacob."

We have now arrived at a period in the history of this congregation, where all the facts and details are perfectly well known to all the present members. It will not be necessary therefore to dwell upon the events of the history farther, except merely to mention the time when the last two pastors entered upon their pastoral duties. The Rev. Edwin H. Nevin, D.D., was called from the Second Reformed Church at Lancaster, to this charge, about Jan. 1st, 1871, and retired on May 1st, 1875. He was succeeded by the present pastor on Nov. 14th, of the same year.

And now the pleasant duty of tracing the history of this congregation is finished. There are those, who pretend that they can find no pleasure or profit in dwelling upon the facts and events that belong to that mighty past, in which all our acts and thoughts are gathered for permanent record.

But surely, many interesting and instructive lessons may be drawn, even from the history of a single congregation. And the century and a half over which this history extends, with the actors and scenes here described, must be of interest, especially to those to whom the interests of this church are now entrusted for safe-keeping.

Reformed Churches in Philadelphia in 1876.

The Race Street Congregation may be truthfully named the mother of nearly all the Reformed Churches in Philadelphia. As a suitable conclusion to this brief history and possibly for use in future reference, we will name the different Reformed Churches in this city, springing from us immediately or remotely, with dates of organization and names of pastors, as nearly as we have been able to ascertain them.

Salem's Reformed Church (German), now worshiping in their fine church edifice at Fairmount avenue and Fourth street.

This congregation was organized in September, 1817, by sixty-seven German members of the Race Street Church, and first worshiped in Old Commissioners' Hall, on Third street. They then erected a church-building in St. John street, below Green street, which they occupied until they removed to their present building in 1873. Pastors: Revs. Frederick W. Van Der Sloot, Henry Bibighaus, D.D., (assisted successively by Christian R. Kessler, Wm. J. Mann, D.D., Chas. Bonekemper,) Adolph Rahn, and John G. Wiehle, D.D.

Christ Reformed Church (English), now worshiping in their elegant church-building, on Green street, near Sixteenth street. Organized on September 15th, 1859, in a public hall, corner of Broad and Spring-Garden streets, with seventeen members, under the auspices of the Race street congregation. They met for the first time in the basement of their new church on Jan. 2d, 1861—building dedicated Christmas-day, 1865. Pastors: Revs. Samuel H. Giesy, D.D., Joseph H. Dubbs and Geo. H. Johnston.

Trinity Reformed Church (English), located in their fine structure of brown stone at Seventh and Oxford streets. Organized in the Hall of American Mechanics, Fourth and George streets, in June, 1867, with a number of members, formerly from the Race Street Church, then living in that vicinity. They entered their new church-building on February 6th, 1870—dedication took place on Easter Sunday, 1872. Rev. D. E. Klopp, D.D., pastor.

Heidelberg Reformed Church (English), was organized on October 11th, 1868, largely with members, formerly connected with the Race Street congregation. Their new chapel, on the N. E. corner of Nineteenth and Oxford streets was dedicated on Jan. 18th, 1874. Rev. W. C. Hendrickson, pastor.

The following named congregations of Philadelphia, are also connected with the Reformed Church in the United States though they do not trace their origin so directly to the Race Street Church:

Zion's (German), Sixth street above Girard avenue; was organized by Rev. Charles Bonekemper, in 1852, with members from the Salem's congregation. Pastors: Rev. Charles Bonekemper and Nicholas Gehr, D.D.

Bethlehem's (German), Kensington. Howard above Thompson street. Organized by Rev. H. A. Friedel, on Oct. 8th, 1852, in Phœnix Hall, on Thompson street below Front, South side. The membership also came largely from the Salem's congregation. Pastors: Revs. H. A. Friedel, J. Gantenbein, G. E. Gramm, J. G. Neuber.

Emanuel's (German), Weisert street, Bridesburg. Organized by Rev. J. G. Neuber, in 1861—church dedicated in 1863. Pastors: Revs. J. G. Neuber, Emanuel Boehringer, John Gantenbein, John C. Beinhauer, J. Dahlman, Sen., Christian Keller.

St. Stephen's (German), Corinthian avenue below Poplar street. Organized in 1864, with fifty members, by Rev. Abraham Romich, the only pastor.

St. Paul's (German), S. E. corner of Seventeenth and Fitzwater streets, was organized in February, 1864. Pastors: Revs. J. C. Hauser, J. Gantenbein, J. Roeck.

St. John's (English), Haverford avenue above Fortieth street. Organized in school-room of Prof. Hastings, at Thirty-fourth street and Powelton avenue, on October 1st, 1865. The congregation built a chapel on Thirty-fifth street above Powelton avenue, the corner-stone of which was laid May 21st, 1866—dedicated on Nov. 4th of the same year. The chapel where they worship at present, was purchased Sept., 1873. Pastors: Revs. Albert G. Dole, George B. Russell, D.D., John G. Noss.

Emanuel's (German), West Philadelphia. Organized by Rev. N. Gehr, D.D., and Licentiate Jacob Dahlman, in the chapel on Story street below Thirty-eighth street; at which time Rev. Jacob Dahlman became the pastor. The congregation built their church at the corner of Baring and Thirty-eighth streets in 1872, and dedicated it on the 18th of May, 1873. Pastor: Rev. Jacob Dahlman.

St. Mark's (German), Fourth and York streets, was organized with 76 members on the 11th of February, 1876, in the chapel where they at present worship—a mission of the Zion's Church.

It is proper to add in this connection, that the First Reformed Church, located at Seventh and Spring Garden streets, and the Second Reformed Church, located on Seventh above Brown street, though connected with another denomination—the Reformed Church in North America—were originally organized with members largely from the old Race Street Church. The circumstances of their organization are given in the preceding history.

Ecclesiastical Connection and Retrospect.

The fact, that the two denominations bearing the Reformed name in this country, come in contact with each other in Philadelphia, has led to some confusion in the past. The church, the history of which is given in full in the preceding pages, has been known as the First Reformed Church of Philadelphia, for nearly one hundred and fifty years. It is also sometimes called the Race Street Reformed Church, because it has occupied the lot on Race street below Fourth street since 1747. Its denominational connection is with the Reformed Church in the United States, (formerly known as the German Reformed Church), having its churches and institutions of various kinds located chiefly in Pennsylvania, Maryland, Ohio and other Southern and Western States. Its sole doctrinal standard, and confession of faith is the Heidelberg Catechism, its government is Presbyterial with a rotating eldership.

The Reformed Church in North America, formerly known as the Reformed Protestant Dutch Church, has its churches in this city at Seventh and Spring Garden, Seventh and Brown, and Tenth and Filbert streets. It is distinguished from the Reformed Church in the United States, by holding as its doctrinal standards the Canons of the Synod of Dort, and the Belgic Confession in connection with the Heidelberg Catechism. Its general locality lies Eastward and Northward in New Jersey, New York and Michigan.

The confusion arising from the similarity of these two denominations, both in name and doctrine, government and custom was a source of difficulty in the earlier history of the Race Street Congregation. We can trace its influence in the controversy of Mr. Boehm with the Moravians and others, in the troubles between Mr. Schlatter and Mr. Steiner, in the difficulty with Mr. Rothenbühler, and in the agitations connected with the change of language. In each case there seems to have been a misunderstanding as to the relation that these Palatinate, or High Dutch congregations of Pennsylvania sustained to the Low Dutch churches in New York, and through them to the Reformed Church of Holland. The pioneer German Reformed ministers were compelled to appeal for aid, and in some cases for ordination, to the only Reformed neighbors they had, the Low Dutch ministry in New York.

A number of interesting papers belonging to the archives of the Collegiate Reformed [Dutch] Church in New York, were translated a few years ago by the Rev. T. W.

Chambers, D. D. They give us a glimpse of the relation subsisting between the two Churches, at an early day, and incidentally confirm the statements we have given regarding the first organization of the Reformed Church here in Philadelphia. They are printed in full in the Mercersburg Review for October, 1876.

From this document it appears that Mr. Boehm arrived in this country as early as the year 1720. Having been Schoolmaster and Foresinger in Worms, a city of Germany, for about seven years, he found a demand for his services as Reader (Voorlezer) upon his arrival here. The Reformed people around him were destitute of the means of grace, and he became a sort of pastor to them, without receiving any compensation for his services. So well did he perform these services for the destitute Reformed people, that they besought him to assume the functions of the ministerial office. This he did in 1725, receiving as compensation only the voluntary contributions of the people.

When Mr. Weiss arrived here, he visited the Skippach congregation, and preached there. This brought him into collision with Mr. Boehm, who had occupied that point in connection with Falkner's Swamp, and White Marsh. Some of the people discredited Mr. Boehm's ministerial acts because he was not ordained, and wished to retain Mr. Weiss as their regular minister. This resulted in an application from Mr. Boehm and his consistories to the ministers of the Dutch Reformed Church in New York for recognition of his former ministerial acts, and for his ordination— dated July, 1728.

The appeal was forwarded to the Classis of Amsterdam, and a favorable answer was returned, dated June 20th, 1729. The ministers in New York were authorized to ordain Mr. Boehm, and recognize the validity of his ministerial acts, upon condition that he, "shall accept the Heidelberg Catechism and all the Doctrinal Standards as the strict rule of his ministry, and will submit to the Church Order of the Synod of Dortrecht." In November of the same year Mr. Boehm with the three Commissioners from his charge repaired to New York, and gave to the ministers there a pledge in writing that they accepted the conditions imposed by the Classis of Amsterdam, and were ready to fulfill them in the name of their respective congregations. This was formally carried out on November 18th, and the ordination took place on the Sunday following—November 23d, 1729.

At this time a reconciliation was effected between Mr. Boehm and Mr. Weiss, who was also present, respecting their troubles at Skippach. The quaint language runs as follows: "After that Do Johan Philips Böhm, had under the persistent pressure of the Reformed High Dutch Congregations at Falkner's Schwamp, Schipback and Wit Marshen, in the year 1725, assumed the office of their minister without ordination according to the usage of the Churches, there arose in 1727, a grievance concerning this, and some in the congregation of Schipback were induced to abstain from Do

Böhm's ministry, and to accept for their accustomed minister, Mr. Georg Michiel Weiss, who had come over from Germany, and was recognized by them as a regularly ordained clergyman, as he was placed over the Reformed High Dutch Congregation in the city of Philadelphia and at Germantown. Since this some estrangement has arisen between them." Mr. Weiss conceded that the Classis had done right in endorsing Mr. Boehm's ministerial acts, and in authorizing his ordination. This resulted in a complete reconciliation, and hearty expressions of fraternal regard between the two ministers were recorded. It is added, "That Do Weiss, declares his heartfelt desire to become subordinate to the Reverend Classis of Amsterdam, and requests the minister's correspondent to write to the Reverend Classis to that effect, and testifies that he is ready and willing to comply with their Church orders when sent over to him. And that Do Weiss also binds himself to endeavor to bring his congregation in Philadelphia and Germantown, into like subordination." As Mr. Weiss never resumed his ministry in Philadelphia, he did not carry out the last named specification of this agreement.

The relation that these two denominations sustained to each other at an early day is only significant to us now as a historical question. Yet it is to be remembered that the series of troubles that befel the Race Street congregation during its early history may have been induced in great part, by these misunderstandings. They were originally organized by Mr. Weiss, as Palatinate Reformed people before he had connected himself with the Church of Holland in any way.* Then Mr. Boehm came, who was thoroughly loyal to the Holland Church,

---

* "Mr. Weiss was sent into this country by the upper consistory, or Classis, of the Palatinate. He came, it seems, with a number of people migrating thence at that time, as the pastor."—*Lives of Fathers*, Vol. 1, p. 266.

From this statement, and the fact mentioned on the preceding page, that Mr. Weiss was recognized at Skippach, in 1727, as a regularly ordained clergyman placed over the Reformed Congregations in Philadelphia and Germantown, it appears that the organization took place here in that year. Or did Mr. Weiss commence services here with his colony in Sept., 1727, without formal organization?

and under his ministry they were called indifferently, Dutch Calvinists, High Dutch Reformed, &c., by the English-speaking people around them. Then Mr. Schlatter came, clothed with extraordinary powers by the Holland Church; and the Steiner movement may have been a reaction against the close rule of the Consistory—this party demanding that a majority of the congregation should decide all questions affecting their interests, by a vote. There seems to have been an old Palatinate party in the congregation, who never could submit gracefully to Hollandish rule. And whenever a new issue presented itself, as in the case of Mr. Schlatter's trouble, or the trial with Mr. Rothenbühler, or the change of language, there would be parties ready to champion either side.

This consideration, taken in connection with the fact of the prominent location occupied by this congregation—on the border line between the denominations—and the conflict, which was unavoidable under the circumstances, respecting the change of language, will go far toward explaining the peculiar troubles in this church. The people here were not more quarrelsome than others, but the circumstances of their history involved them in repeated trials.

Concluding Reflections.

From this hight of American antiquity the venerable Race Street Reformed Church looks down upon the passing scenes and wonders of our national centennial. She has safely passed through the periods of trial and danger experienced during the times of the first settlement of this country, the Revolutionary conflict, the war of 1812, and our final struggle for national existence. All the changing tides of thought and life and feeling, that have flowed through our country's history, have been reflected here in the changing phases of this church organization. In her internal conflicts also, she presents a counterpart—by her throes in government during her early history, and in her later struggles to change the language of her worship, she was moved by the tides in the affairs of our country settling, gradually, toward the permanent American form, and preparing for this great Centennial Jubilee. May her interests not suffer in our keeping, nor her history be tarnished by our faithlessness, or lack of Christian liberality and devotion!

It should be a matter of rejoicing to the Reformed Church at large, that this congregation with all its trials and difficulties, reaching through its whole history nearly, has been preserved until the present time with a good degree of strength and hope for the future. The history of the denomination, especially in its earlier phases centers here, where the first Synod was organized in 1747, and where the Tercentenary Convention was held, in 1863. And on this account and for other reasons, many members of the Reformed Church should feel the deepest interest in her welfare.